FOCUS ON FORMULA ONE

FORMULA ONE

GRAND PRIX RACES

BY ANTHONY K. HEWSON

An Imprint of Abdo Publishing
abdobooks.com

abdobooks.com

Published by Abdo Publishing, a division of ABDO, PO Box 398166, Minneapolis, Minnesota 55439.

Printed in the United States of America, North Mankato, Minnesota.
052023
092023

Cover Photo: Eric Alonso/Getty Images Sport/Getty Images
Interior Photos: Mario Renzi/Formula 1/Getty Images, 4; Jakub Porzycki/NurPhoto/Getty Images, 6; Darron Cummings/Pool AP/AP Images, 9; Hoch Zwei/picture-alliance/dpa/AP Images, 11; Pascal Rondeau/Getty Images Sport/Getty Images, 12; Darren Heath/Hulton Archive/Getty Images, 14–15; Grand Prix Photo/Hulton Archive/Getty Images, 17; Andy Hone/Motorsport Images/Sipa USA/AP Images, 19; Brendan Smialowski/AFP/AP Images, 20–21; Gongora/NurPhoto/Getty Images, 22; Dan Mullan/Formula 1/Getty Images, 24; Alessio De Marco/LiveMedia/NurPhoto/Getty Images, 26; Alex Pantling/Formula 1/Getty Images, 28–29

Editor: Charlie Beattie
Series Designer: Michael J. Williams

Library of Congress Control Number: 2022949092

Publisher's Cataloging-in-Publication Data

Names: Hewson, Anthony K., author.
Title: Formula one grand prix races / by Anthony K. Hewson
Description: Minneapolis, Minnesota: Abdo Publishing Company, 2024 | Series: Focus on formula one | Includes online resources and index.
Identifiers: ISBN 9781098290740 (lib. bdg.) | ISBN 9781098276928 (ebook)
Subjects: LCSH: Formula One automobiles--Juvenile literature. | Grand Prix racing--Juvenile literature. | Sports car racing--Juvenile literature. | Automobiles, Racing--History--Juvenile literature.
Classification: DDC 796.72--dc23

TABLE OF

CONTENTS

Lewis Hamilton hops into his car before a qualifying run at the 2022 Abu Dhabi Grand Prix.

CHAPTER ONE

A GRAND WEEKEND

Lewis Hamilton is all alone on the track. Just a few corners remain. If he can keep it up, Hamilton will take the checkered flag. The British driver pushes his Mercedes hard, testing the limits of the track. He crosses the finish line in first place.

However, it's still only Saturday. The race isn't until the next afternoon. Hamilton has secured first place in qualifying, a competition held before the race to determine the starting order. Qualifying is just one part of a Grand Prix weekend. A typical racing weekend includes practice on Friday, qualifying on Saturday, and the race on Sunday.

Racing teams get three practice sessions to fine-tune their cars for qualifying and the race. The first two sessions last 90 minutes each. Saturday morning features the final one-hour practice session.

There are three qualifying sessions. All 20 cars in the Formula One grid get 18 minutes in the first qualifying session (Q1). They are ranked based on the fastest time over one full lap. There are no

Hamilton qualified in fifth position at Abu Dhabi in 2022.

limits on how many cars can be on the track at one time. But drivers try to go out when there are no cars close in front of them so they can go as fast as possible.

SPRINT RACES

Sometimes, a Formula One Grand Prix weekend will feature a short race between qualifying and the actual Grand Prix. This is known as a sprint race. Its starting order is set by qualifying. The finishing order of the sprint race is then the starting order for the Grand Prix.

The car's setup for qualifying is different than the setup for a race. For example, a car can be much lighter and faster because it does not need a full load of fuel. It's all about speed at this point.

The five slowest cars are eliminated after Q1. The second qualifying session, or Q2, lasts for 15 minutes with the same rules. Again the five slowest cars are eliminated. Q3 lasts 12 minutes, and the fastest driver at the end of Q3 gets to start first in Sunday's race. That spot is known as pole position. The rest of the starting order follows the qualifying rankings.

THE RACE

All Grand Prix races are roughly the same distance. No matter how long the track, each race is a minimum of 190 miles (306 km) long. Whichever lap covers the 190th mile (306th km) is the final lap.

However, the races themselves vary a great deal. Formula One is a truly global sport. For example, the 2022 calendar featured 23 races in 21 different countries. Those tracks were very different in length, number of corners, top speed, and other qualities. Teams use practice time to dial in the exact race setup they need.

Formula One straights, like this one at the US Grand Prix in Austin, Texas, cannot be more than 1.2 miles (2 km) long.

DIFFERENT TRACKS

Tracks fall into two major categories. Some are high downforce tracks. Downforce is air pushing the car onto the track. High downforce tracks place an emphasis on taking corners well and overall handling. Other courses are power tracks. Those feature longer straight sections where speed is most important.

Teams must be careful to build cars that can excel on both types of tracks. For example, a car that is set up with too little downforce will be harder to control. But using too much downforce can slow down a car on power-track straightaways. Balancing these two extremes is the battle Formula One teams fight each weekend.

The way tracks are built varies too. Some tracks are built specifically to be racetracks. Other temporary tracks are built using public streets that regular cars drive on the rest of the year. Each type has its own unique look.

The variety of different tracks is one thing fans love about Formula One. Every Grand Prix is truly different. And each one offers a special thrill throughout the season.

The Circuit Gilles-Villeneuve in Montreal is one of the shortest Grand Prix tracks on the Formula One schedule. Each lap covers roughly 2.7 miles (4.3 km).

The narrow streets of Monaco take racers past fans on balconies and yachts.

CHAPTER TWO

HITTING THE STREETS

Street circuits take Formula One to the heart of some of the world's most famous cities. Races are often run on public streets. That means people can typically watch from public squares or the balconies of their homes.

These settings create dramatic spectacles. Street circuits have some downsides, though. Because the streets are usually surrounded by buildings, there is not much space on the side of the road for any car that spins off the track. A public street can also be narrow, meaning passing could be difficult.

Turn 6 at Monaco is known as the Grand Hotel Hairpin.

MONACO

One street course that features both extremes is the Monaco Grand Prix. Monaco is a tiny principality surrounded by southern France and the Mediterranean Sea. Its Grand Prix is one of auto racing's most famous events. Though Formula One did not start until 1950, racers have competed at Monaco since 1929. And while cars have gotten bigger and more powerful, the race

has barely changed. Three-time world champion Nelson Piquet once compared the race to riding a bicycle around a living room.

Monaco's narrow streets and tight corners pose a unique challenge for today's drivers. Turn 6 is the tightest and slowest corner on the tour schedule. Racers must take Turn 6 at around 30 miles per hour (48 km/h), with the steering wheel cranked all the way to the left.

Passing can be difficult in Monaco. Not a single pass was made during the 2003 Grand Prix. There is also no space on the sides of the track for damaged cars to move onto. If Monaco were not already on the Formula One calendar, it would not meet today's safety requirements.

The layout of the track has led to some memorable crashes over the years. In 1965 Australian Paul Hawkins crashed his Lotus into the harbor and had to swim to safety. Monaco resident Ayrton Senna crashed out of the

THE BEST DAY IN RACING

Monaco is traditionally held on the last Sunday in May. It shares that day with two other major auto races. IndyCar holds the Indianapolis 500, one of the most famous races in the United States. NASCAR holds its 600-mile (966-km) race at Charlotte Motor Speedway. For auto-racing fans, it's the greatest day of the year.

Paul Hawkins's car was hauled out of the harbor in Monaco after he crashed into the water during the 1965 Grand Prix.

1988 race. He simply got out of his car and walked to his apartment.

The Monaco experience is about more than just racing. The race's long history attracts fans from all over the world. Some arrive by boat, tying up their luxurious yachts in the harbor to watch the race from there. The historic Grand Prix has also been a favorite of many drivers, including

"Mr. Monaco" Graham Hill. The Englishman won the event five times during the 1960s.

OTHER STREET COURSES

For many years, Monaco was the only street circuit regularly on the Formula One schedule. But eventually more street courses were created. The Marina Bay Street Circuit in Singapore has become one of Formula One's premier events since debuting in 2008.

That year Marina Bay made history as the first night race in Formula One. The circuit's bumpy public streets and 23 corners make even one lap physically demanding for drivers. Singapore's hot and humid weather creates additional challenges.

Singapore offers a unique fan experience. In Turn 18, the racers pass underneath the grandstand. Fans can watch them from above.

Cars fly down the main straight at the 2022 Singapore Grand Prix.

The Miami Grand Prix was one of 15 races Max Verstappen won during the 2022 season.

The Baku City Circuit in Azerbaijan debuted in 2016. The circuit passes some of the most historic sites in the country's capital, Baku. One series of turns is built around a medieval castle.

Baku is another tricky race for drivers. It has tight corners like Monaco but also one of the longest straights on the schedule. Teams have

to balance the car correctly to be able to handle both elements.

A new street circuit made its debut in Miami in 2022. Red Bull's Max Verstappen won its first race. Another street course was added for 2023 in Las Vegas.

Drivers Sergio Perez, *left,* and Charles Leclerc drive side by side during the 2022 British Grand Prix.

CHAPTER THREE

AROUND THE CIRCUIT

Most of the tracks on the Formula One calendar are used only for racing. But in the early days, tracks weren't always built with the sport in mind. One of Formula One's most famous racecourses had a very different beginning.

World War II (1939–45) had a devastating effect on racing across Europe. Many tracks were totally destroyed. Afterward, drivers searched for anyplace they could find to hold a race. In England they found an old air force base called Silverstone. No longer needed for the war effort,

Cars racing at Silverstone enter the Abbey turn from the Hamilton Straight, which is named after driver Lewis Hamilton.

the pavement of the airfield proved to be a perfect spot.

The Silverstone Circuit held its first race in 1948. At that time, Formula One was still being planned. The English track was chosen to host the very first Grand Prix in 1950. Even King George VI of England came out to watch.

The early track layout was wide open, allowing for fast speeds. Changes over the years have added turns and made the track a technical challenge for drivers. The blend of flat-out speed and tight cornering makes Silverstone one of the most beloved circuits on the calendar. Each year it attracts around 350,000 people for race weekend.

The track's famous corners and straights all have names well known to fans. Turn 1 is named "Abbey" after nearby Luffield Abbey, which has stood for roughly 1,000 years. The Wellington Straight is named after the Wellington bombers that used to call the airfield home.

MONZA

When it comes to speed, Monza in Italy is king. Teams plan for low downforce at Monza, as its long straights mean lots of time at full throttle. It is also the home of Ferrari, so many passionate fans turn out for races in the company's famous red color.

SPA-FRANCORCHAMPS

One track began life as a street circuit but now is an enclosed course. Spa-Francorchamps in Belgium opened in 1921 as a winding 10-mile (16-km) course. It was still that way when Formula One arrived in 1950. Back then Spa was wide open, thrilling, and dangerous. The Masta Kink was a quick left-right corner taken at nearly full speed. Former world champion Jackie Stewart once described it as the most dangerous corner in auto racing.

Spa-Francorchamps is one of four tracks used during Formula One's first season in 1950 that are still on the schedule each year.

Spa was straightened out and shortened to half its original length in 1979. But it's still the longest track in Formula One. The course covers a huge plot of land with many elevation changes. It can be raining on parts of the track and dry in other spots. That makes tire selection a tricky challenge for teams. Spa's weather can also ruin a race weekend. In 2021 the race was reduced to two laps because of rain. It was the shortest Grand Prix ever run.

Spa's track is located in a remote forest. Many visitors to the race actually camp at the site. Some of them put their tents up right by the track.

Spa features one of the most famous corners in racing. *Eau Rouge* is Turn 2 on the track. Its name means "red water," inspired by the creek that runs nearby. Cars approach Eau Rouge running downhill at full speed. They then take the quick

left turn. That is followed by a steep uphill turn to the right. Taking the turn at maximum speed without crashing is one of the toughest tests in racing.

Several cars make their way around the Eau Rouge corner at the 2022 Belgian Grand Prix at Spa.

Formula One fans all have their favorite tracks. That's what makes the sport so exciting from week to week. Each Grand Prix is unique and contains thrills unlike anything else in sports.

GLOSSARY

checkered flag
A black-and-white-checked flag that signals a race is over.

cornering
The ability of cars to go around a corner.

enclosed
Closed in or fenced off.

grid
The full field of drivers in a race.

handling
The measure of how well a car is able to be controlled by a driver.

lap
A single complete circuit of a racetrack.

principality
An area of land that is governed by a prince or princess.

straight
A section of a racetrack without any corners or turns.

throttle
The power applied to a vehicle.

MORE INFORMATION

BOOKS

Hewson, Anthony K. *The History of Formula One.* Minneapolis, MN: Abdo Publishing, 2024.

Hustad, Douglas. *Innovations in Auto Racing*. Minneapolis, MN: Abdo Publishing, 2022.

Rule, Heather. *GOATs of Auto Racing*. Minneapolis, MN: Abdo Publishing, 2022.

ONLINE RESOURCES

To learn more about Formula One Grand Prix races, please visit **abdobooklinks.com** or scan this QR code. These links are routinely monitored and updated to provide the most current information available.

INDEX

ABOUT THE AUTHOR

Anthony K. Hewson is a freelance writer originally from San Diego. He and his wife now live in the San Francisco Bay Area with their two dogs.